THE STORY OF

HENRY HUDSON,
Master Explorer

D0957420

THE STORY OF

HENRY HUDSON,
Master Explorer

BY ERIC WEINER

ILLUSTRATED BY MARIE DeJOHN

A YEARLING BOOK

ABOUT THIS BOOK

The events described in this book are true. They have been carefully researched and excerpted from authentic autobiographies, writings, and commentaries. No part of this biography has been fictionalized.

To learn more about Henry Hudson, ask your librarian to recommend other fine books you might read.

Dedicated to Cherie

Published by
Dell Publishing
a division of
Bantam Doubleday Dell Publishing Group, Inc.
666 Fifth Avenue
New York, New York 10103

ISBN: 0-440-40513-0

Published by arrangement with Parachute Press, Inc.
Printed in the United States of America
October 1991
10 9 8 7 6 5 4 3 2 1
CWO

Contents

Introduction

Imagine living in England, over four hundred years ago. What was life like?

For one thing, people dressed very differently. Both girls and boys wore hats decorated with plumes of feathers. Young boys wore a kind of skirt that reached the floor. Older boys wore baggy knee-length pants and stockings!

Dressing up that way may sound like fun, but life back then was a lot harder than it is today. No one had natural gas to warm his or her home, or electricity to light the way. Houses had no plumbing, no running water, and no bathrooms. Even soap was a very rare thing, an item of great luxury.

A person could barely survive on products made only in England. At that time, the English had to rely on trade with other countries to fill many of their basic needs.

The trouble was, some of the most important products of all, the real "treasures," could be found only in countries such as China that lay halfway around the world.

In the 1500s, there were no cars, no airplanes, no ocean liners, and no trains. The quickest way to get to the Orient was in a tiny wooden boat, with room for only about twenty people.

The route to China was thousands of miles long. It led all the way around the Cape of Good Hope, the southern tip of Africa. That trip took two or three years! Along the way, ocean storms dashed many of the little ships against the rocks, and hundreds of sailors lost their lives.

All over Europe, kings, queens, and merchants kept asking themselves the same question: Was there a *shorter*, safer route? The country that found a faster way to China would become very rich. A shortcut would let merchants bring back many more boatloads of spices, and at a much lower cost.

Today, we take spices such as sugar and pepper for granted. But in the 1500's, sugar and pepper were as rare as gold. In those days, people had no refrigerators. Europeans needed spices to keep their meat from spoiling. Spices also covered up the taste of meat that was going bad.

Also, people living in the 1500s rarely bathed. Queen Isabella of Spain once claimed that she had taken only two baths in her entire life! Wearing spicy ointments and perfumes was the only way for most people to smell fresh.

Not only were Europeans willing to pay a fortune for spices, there were other reasons to find shortcuts to other worlds, too. There were lands to conquer, lands that people in countries like England, France, and Spain hadn't yet explored. Whoever discovered these lands and uncovered their hidden treasures could make an entire country rich!

And so, the treasure hunt began.

To find a shorter route to China, merchants hired some of the most daring men the world has ever known—men like Sebastian Cabot, Christopher Columbus, Vasco da Gama, Ferdinand Magellan, and Sir Francis Drake. Again and again, these brave sea explorers risked, and sometimes lost, their lives on the high seas.

With no accurate maps to tell them where to go or what to expect, these explorers were almost sailing blind. They didn't know what rough seas they would find, or what strange countries they would land in. Maybe they would meet cannibals, or sea dragons! Or perhaps they would fall into a violent whirlpool that could suck a boat to the bottom of the sea! No one knew for sure.

For over one hundred years, explorers searched for a shortcut to those spices. They made many valuable discoveries along the way. Columbus, for instance, had found a huge land mass blocking his way to China—he had discovered America. Drake proved that the Earth was round—he sailed all the way around the globe!

Still, by 1607, the grand prize had yet to be discovered. No one had found a short route to the treasure. Most of the countries of Europe were giving up the hunt. They had spent too much money, lost too many men.

But in England one sea captain remained hopeful. He still believed that a shortcut existed—and he believed that he was the man to find it!

The captain's name was Henry Hudson. In his last four voyages, he would change history forever.

Heading for the North Pole

By the 1550s, the famous British explorer Sebastian Cabot had grown too old for the hardships of sea. He had spent most of his life searching for a shortcut to China. To keep his dream alive, he brought together a group of merchants to form the Muscovy Company.

The Muscovy Company's merchants traded with Russia for valuables such as furs, animal hides, and timber. These trades brought in the money that paid for the company's riskier trips. But the main goal of the Muscovy Company was to find the shortcut to China.

Henry Hudson was raised on this dream. His grandfather and his father both worked for Cabot's company. At an early age, Hudson was hearing about the company's quest for the riches of the Far East.

Henry Hudson later became one of the

most famous explorers of all time. But we don't know much about his early years. Where did he come from? What was his childhood like? How did he become such a skilled sea captain? No one knows for sure. The first known record of Hudson is a ship's logbook, which Henry kept on a journey to the North Pole.

Perhaps someday an old sea chest will turn up, with another logbook that tells us more about Hudson. In the meantime, historians have tried to piece together the puzzle of his past.

The lure of the sea was strong for Hudson. No one knows for sure, but it is believed that as a young teenager, Henry began shipping out on dangerous ocean trips.

At first, Henry had to serve as a cabin boy. This wasn't an easy job, but it was the only way to learn sailing. At school, Henry had studied subjects such as arithmetic, grammar, Latin, Greek, and debating—but there was nothing to tell him how to guide a ship through a storm.

Cabin boys ran errands for the captain and crew. They also had to keep watch with all the other sailors. That meant spending long night hours on the dark, windy deck, ready to shout out when they saw a light or another ship.

In return for all this work, cabin boys were paid only with food. In those days, the food onboard a ship was often foul—cold, salty meat and moldy bread. Like the rest of the sailors, the cabin boys had to sleep in little hutches set up on the lower deck.

But if a boy wanted to become a sailor, this was the only way to begin. Once they reached the age of sixteen, cabin boys could become apprentices. Then they would begin to learn the art of sailing. To become sailors, boys had to serve as apprentices for seven long years.

In this way, Henry slowly worked his way up the ranks. He must have become an excellent seaman, for one day the Muscovy Company made him a ship's master, or captain.

By 1607, Henry Hudson was a married man with three sons: Oliver, Richard, and John. On Hudson's next trip, he would bring John along. John would begin his sailing career as a cabin boy, just as his father had done before him. Now father and son would sail for the Muscovy Company together.

On April 19, 1607, Henry Hudson and his crew visited St. Ethelburga's Church in London. Sailors were a common sight in this church. It was right near the docks. Mariners often came there to pray for a safe trip.

But these sailors were preparing for one of the most dangerous sea voyages in history. No one had ever tried what they were about to try. Hudson was planning to sail right past the North Pole.

He knew that there would be ice in his way. But he also knew that in summer there were long hours of sunshine at the Pole. Like many people in his day, Hudson thought the sun would melt most of this ice.

He believed there would be a clear passage to get his ship through. From there, he hoped, it would be a short trip to China.

After praying, Captain Hudson and his crew of twelve boarded their tiny ship, the *Hopewell*. The anchor was raised, and Hudson steered his ship down the Thames River. They were on their way to the North Pole.

For the first month and a half, the weather was good. The sun shone. The winds kept blowing in the right direction—north. Then, suddenly, the bright sun disappeared. Freezing winds began to blow from the east. With the winds came thick fog.

"Our sails did freeze," Hudson wrote in the ship's log. The winds were so powerful, it seemed as if they might rip the sails apart.

But Hudson kept sailing north. The *Hopewell* hugged the eastern coast of Greenland. The sailors were searching for a waterway that would lead them through the island. But they were barely able to see in the fog, and could only make out the hazy outline of the shore.

High up, near the top of the ship's main mast, was a perch for the lookout. It was called the crow's nest. The sailors took turns standing there, trying to peer ahead through the blinding mist.

James Young was in the crow's nest when the fog broke. Suddenly he now saw Greenland in all its glory. Jutting toward them was a long, narrow piece of land. Behind this cape was an endless row of beautiful snow-capped mountains. Young shouted the news to the men below. In his honor, Hudson named the site Young's Cape.

But Captain Hudson had more on his mind than naming new lands. He wanted to get past the Pole to warmer waters. Unable to find a waterway that led through Greenland, he turned the *Hopewell* back toward the open sea.

From time to time, the sailors had spotted bears romping on the icy shore. They killed and ate several. But they soon found that unsalted bear meat caused them terrible stomachaches.

After that, the *Hopewell*'s crew stuck to fishing to bring in extra food. But fishing this far north was sometimes dangerous. By accident, one of Hudson's sailors caught a whale!

Hudson wrote about it in the ship's log: "One of our company having a hook and line overboard to try for fish, a whale came under the keel of our ship. Yet by God's mercy we had no harm, but the loss of the hook and three parts of the line."

On June 27, Hudson found his way blocked once again. This time he had reached a group of islands now known as Spitsbergen. Here the men saw another astonishing sight— huge gray whales. It seemed as though there were *hundreds* of them.

The whales swam together in large groups known as pods, spouting and diving. Hudson carefully charted the spots where the whales gathered. He knew he had made an important find.

By this time it was July. That was a month that the English sailors thought of as warm. But not now. They suffered from constant cold. They met with such bad weather that Hudson referred to the ice and fog as "our troublesome neighbors."

As bad as the weather seemed then, it would soon get worse. On the morning of July 27, the men awoke to fog as usual, but at least the water was calm. A few hours later, the sea seemed to boil as towering waves crashed down on the deck.

Then a frightening sound was heard. Just ahead, a giant piece of ice had broken off from a vast ice mass. This process, known as calving, is how icebergs are formed. The iceberg had calved right in front of the *Hopewell*! Powerful winds were blowing the ship right into the berg!

Quickly, Hudson ordered his crew to lower the ship's rowboat into the water. As fast as they could, the men tied a rope from rowboat to ship. The sailors crowded into the little boat and rowed as hard as they could: They were actually trying to tug the ship out of the way.

But the oars were too short. No matter how hard the men rowed, the *Hopewell* still headed

straight for the ice. In another moment, the ship would be smashed to bits.

Just then, the wind changed its course. The *Hopewell* was blown out of the path of the iceberg. The ship was saved!

After this near miss, Henry Hudson had to make a hard decision. He was running low on supplies. The wind and fog were only getting worse. Sadly, the captain decided it was time to admit defeat. He would have to find the shortcut on another voyage. He gave the order to turn around, and the *Hopewell* headed for home.

The *Hopewell* had reached a latitude of 80° 23′— about 575 nautical miles from the North Pole. That was closer than anyone had ever been before.

Hudson's record would stand unbroken for 166 years.

The *Hopewell* Meets a Mermaid

The *Hopewell* returned to London in the middle of September, with its whole crew safe. Henry Hudson knew that he had been farther north than any other explorer. But he hadn't found the shortcut. In his mind, the trip was a failure.

Hudson's bosses at the Muscovy Company felt differently. The captain's charts told them where to find thousands of whales at Spitsbergen. Whale blubber could be used to make many important products such as soap and oil. With Hudson's maps to guide them, the Muscovy Company hoped for great profits.

During the next few years, large fleets of whaling ships would hunt at Spitsbergen. Henry Hudson would come to be known as the father of English whaling. But right now Hudson had only one thing on his mind. He wanted to find the shortcut to the East. The Muscovy Company was very pleased with the results of his last trip. They would gladly pay for another.

But he couldn't sail until spring. Hudson put that time to good use. All winter he planned and prepared for his next voyage. He studied maps and gathered his crew. This time he would sail with fifteen men, three more than before. But only a few sailors from his previous trip were willing to come again.

Hudson didn't plan on sailing straight to the North Pole this time. He had plotted a route *around* the Pole to the east. But this would mean just as much ice, fog, and freezing winds as before. Most of the sailors from the first trip had seen enough—they didn't feel the danger was worth the small amount of pay they would receive.

Old Robert Juet had sailed with Hudson before, and he signed on again as first mate. This meant he was next in command under the captain. Among his duties, he had to enforce discipline among the crew. For cabin boy, Hudson chose a familiar face—his young son John.

Hudson's loyal carpenter, Philip Staffe, also agreed to return. Carpenters had a key job on sea voyages. If the wooden ship was damaged in a storm, it would be up to Staffe to lead the repairs.

Hudson would again sail in the *Hopewell*, but this time, he got a better shallop. That was the ship's rowboat. Henry was careful to find a shallop with much longer oars. He wanted to be better prepared for icebergs.

He had good reason to be cautious. He planned to follow the route used by Sir Hugh Willoughby. Like Hudson, Captain Willoughby had sailed for the Muscovy Company. In 1554, his ship had frozen in the ice in the Arctic Ocean. Months later, Russian fishermen had boarded the ice-bound boat. They found the captain sitting in his cabin, pen in hand, his log book open. Willoughby had frozen to death as he tried to record the final details of his journey. Every member of the crew had also perished.

On Friday, April 22, 1608, the *Hopewell* raised anchor and pulled away from London's St. Katharine's Docks. Another adventure had begun.

It was now late May. The *Hopewell* was sailing through icy waters off the coast of Norway. Again the ship faced heavy fog and fierce cold.

Five sailors fell ill, including the carpenter, Philip Staffe. They soon became too sick to leave their bunks.

At last the weather cleared. Two weeks of bright sun cured the sick men and cheered everyone's spirits. Meanwhile, the *Hopewell* continued north. The sailors knew that more hardships lay ahead.

The real trouble started in early June. One day the ship found its path blocked by an ice-filled sea. Hudson, a masterful sailor, was able to steer through the icebergs. But as he sailed on, more and more ice seemed to appear all around. Hudson looked back. Behind them, the ice was beginning to pack together. Any minute now, the *Hopewell* would be trapped, and they would freeze like Captain Willoughby and his crew.

Hudson tried to turn the little ship around. But the bitter wind had frozen the rigging. As Hudson yelled instructions, the sailors' hands slipped off the icy ropes. Large boulders of ice slammed against the ship's sides. Finally, Hudson was able to lead the ship back out of danger. But the ice had badly scraped the *Hopewell*'s hull.

For a couple of weeks now, the crew had

seen nothing but fog. Then, in mid-June, two crew members saw something very different.

It happened in the morning, as one sailor was looking over the ship's side. Suddenly he spotted a strange creature swimming nearby. He cried out, and another sailor joined him.

"By that time she was come close to the ship's side," Hudson wrote. She was "looking earnestly on the men." Then a wave splashed over her, and she was gone. "From the navel upward, her back and breasts were like a woman's, as they say that saw her. Her body as big as one of us. Her skin was very white. She had long hair hanging down behind, of color black.

"In her going down they saw her tail, which was like the tail of a porpoise, and speckled like a mackerel. Their names that saw her were Thomas Hille and Robert Rayner."

The sailors were sure they had seen a mermaid. No one knows what it might actually have been. Hudson didn't see it himself—he only reported what his sailors told him.

Perhaps Hille and Rayner saw a fish they didn't recognize. With so much fog it was hard to see clearly, and for weeks there had been nothing out there except ice. But it was exciting

for the men to imagine they had seen a mermaid, whatever it really was.

In the next few days, the crew saw no more mermaids, only huge amounts of ice. To play it safe, Hudson sailed a little way south. Here, he hoped, the ice would be less heavy. As they sailed south, the sailors suddenly found that they had a lot of company. All around the ship floated a vast herd of walruses. The tusked creatures lay on tiny islands of ice, sunning themselves and taking naps. The sight of the strange sailboat didn't seem to frighten them.

The *Hopewell*'s crew needed food. In addition, walrus hides and tusks were valuable. Hudson sent the entire crew out in the shallop to hunt, while he and his young son John stayed aboard to guard the ship.

Whenever the shallop rowed close to a walrus, the animal simply dived into the water. The men were able to catch only one walrus. The rest of the huge herd just swam away. The men were left disappointed—and hungry.

On July 2, the sailor in the crow's nest sang out with exciting news. Up ahead was the mouth of a large river. This looked like the passage Hudson had been searching for. He began to guide the *Hopewell* up the river. But just then, a white mountain appeared from out of the fog.

It was an iceberg, and it was gliding right toward them! The berg was huge. Hudson wrote that it was "very fearful to look on." He ordered all hands on deck.

The new long oars Hudson had put in the shallop were no help. There was simply no time to get the rowboat in the water. Instead, Hudson had everyone grab an oar, a spar, or some other weapon. For hours the weary sailors held the berg away from their ship with these poles.

Finally, at around six o'clock, they were able to push their ship out of the iceberg's path. They watched, exhausted, as the white mountain floated harmlessly past.

Now the river lay open before them. And beyond? The men hoped they would find the riches of China.

Hudson sent a few men ahead in the shallop to explore. In a few hours they came back with bad news. After twenty miles the river became too shallow for the larger ship. This was not the passage east.

By now, the crew was sick of ice, fog, cold, and danger. They wanted to turn back while they still could. But Hudson wanted to keep going. He wanted to return to the western side of the Pole, to search the same area he had explored on his last voyage. If they could just get through the polar region, he said, the weather would warm up quickly.

The crew wanted no part of it. As they saw the matter, Hudson had the most to gain by going on. He would get a big reputation and a lot of money. But they would get almost nothing—only risks and hard work. It looked as though they were about to mutiny.

Finally, Hudson gave in. He would sail back to England. But the men still weren't satisfied. What if Hudson made trouble for them when they returned? Would he say that they had refused to follow his orders?

To calm them down, Hudson signed a special certificate. It said that he was turning back of his own free will—not because of a mutiny.

If the men had known Henry Hudson better, they wouldn't have worried. The captain wasn't interested in making things hard for his sailors. His only goal was to keep on searching.

A Master Without a Ship

Hudson returned to England in the fall of 1608. But this time the Muscovy Company was not at all pleased with the results of his voyage. He hadn't found his way to China. And he hadn't found anything else of interest to the Company, either.

The directors of the company had decided to give up their costly search for a shortcut. Maybe such a passage simply didn't exist.

Hudson remained sure that it did. But he couldn't sail alone. He needed people with money to provide him with a ship and a crew. If a daring group like the Muscovy Company was giving up the search, who would back him?

He didn't have to wait long for the answer. A few weeks later, Hudson received a letter from the Dutch East India Company in Amsterdam, Holland.

Trading with the Orient was this company's main business. If another country found a shorter passage to China, the Dutch East India Company would be ruined. Obviously, the Dutch merchants were eager to be the first to find a shorter route.

Word of Hudson's bold exploring had spread to many countries. As far as the Dutch East India Company was concerned, Henry Hudson sounded like the perfect man for the job. They asked him to come to Amsterdam and meet with them right away.

Hudson stayed in London a little longer to attend the christening of his newborn granddaughter. Then he set sail. When he arrived in Holland, he found himself in an exciting, bustling seaport. The noisy marketplace looked much like London. But here Captain Hudson could smell rare spices and perfumes—those glorious treasures Dutch sailors had brought back from China.

In a meeting with the Dutch merchants, Hudson made his proposal. He would travel along the northeastern route he had just tried, but this time he would not turn back until the passage was found.

His proposal impressed the Dutch. But they also had doubts. In 1596 Willem Barents, a Dutch explorer, had tried a northeastern route. His crew had been ice-bound in the Arctic Ocean for an entire winter. Sick with cold and hunger, Barents had died at sea. The rest of the crew barely survived.

So the merchants told Hudson that he would have to wait. In March, all the directors of the Dutch East India Company would hold a meeting. If Hudson would come back then, he could repeat his proposal. Then all the directors would decide together.

March! If his plans for a new trip didn't begin until March, it would be too late to sail that year. Although disappointed, Hudson decided not to return to London right away. As it turned out, it was lucky he stayed.

There was someone else in Amsterdam Hudson wanted to see. The man's name was Peter Plancius, and he was one of the top geographers and mapmakers of his day.

Plancius was a firm believer that a new way to China could be found. Together, Hudson and Plancius studied maps and globes, searching for possible shortcuts.

While he and the geographer charted new routes, some very powerful people were talking about Henry Hudson and his voyages. The English explorer had become the talk of the royal court of France!

King Henry IV of France sent secret orders to his ambassador in Holland, Pierre Jeannin. The King wanted him to locate an explorer who might find a shorter passage to China. Jeannin, in turn, sent for Isaac Le Maire, a rich Dutch merchant who had traded with China for years. Le Maire told Jeannin that he knew the perfect sea captain for France—a skillful and fearless Englishman named Henry Hudson.

At the ambassador's request, Le Maire then met secretly with Hudson. Jeannin wanted to know how much a trip would cost, and whether Hudson would be willing to sail for France.

Through Le Maire, Hudson told the Frenchman how much money he would need. Jeannin then met secretly with Plancius, the mapmaker. Did Plancius believe there was a quicker, northern route to China? Yes, Plancius told Jeannin, he was sure there was.

Le Maire, Plancius, and Hudson convinced the French ambassador that a trip was worth the price. Jeannin wrote to his king recommending that France hire Hudson at once. He ended his letter by saying that France had almost nothing to lose. "Even though nothing should come of the plan, it will always be a laudable thing," wrote Jeannin. "And the regret will not be great, since so little is risked."

Although Le Maire's meeting with Hudson was supposed to be secret, word soon leaked out. The merchants of the Dutch East India Company guessed what France was up to, and they sent for Hudson at once. They had changed their minds, they said. They no longer needed to wait until March for the meeting of all the directors. They would make the decision themselves, and Hudson would sail for them. They might have added, "And *not* for France!"

With the help of an interpreter, Hudson and the merchants quickly agreed to a contract. Hudson would receive only 800 guilders for leading the voyage, but if he perished at sea his widow would get 200 guilders more. Also, he insisted that the Dutch pay his family's expenses while he was away. All in all, it was very little money. But what mattered to Hudson was that he would be sailing—and searching—once more.

The Dutch merchants put something else into his contract—the exact route. Hudson was to try for a passage to the *east* of the North Pole. He was *not* to try any other routes. If this failed, he was to come straight back. And if he broke the contract, he would risk losing his pay.

Hudson agreed. But he already had in mind a bold plan for breaking the agreement. Success as an explorer meant far more to him than 800 guilders!

Later, King Henry sent word to Jeannin to offer Hudson 4,000 crowns—a much better offer. But it came too late. Hudson had already been hired by the Dutch. (In his place, the French hired a less skillful explorer. This French voyage began in May, a month after Hudson's, and it failed completely.)

On January 8, 1609, two Dutch merchants, Dirk Van Os and J. Poppe, signed Hudson's contract for the Dutch East India Company. Henry Hudson added his signature to both copies. His most famous voyage was about to begin.

Hudson got right down to business. He needed a ship, supplies, and a crew. It would take three months to prepare for the new voyage.

Hudson would sail in the *Half Moon*. This ship weighed eight tons, and was a little less than sixty feet long. At its widest point, it measured only sixteen feet across. Hudson was satisfied, though. He believed he could steer this small ship through storms and ice.

The captain would have liked an English crew. But the merchants insisted that at least half the sailors be Dutch. For the key crew members, however, Hudson tried to hire sailors he knew.

He sent for old Robert Juet, of Limehouse, in England. "The ancient man," his fellow sailors called him. Hudson also summoned his son John, who was now old enough to stop serving as cabin boy. On this voyage he would begin his training as a sailor.

Hudson spent many more hours studying maps with Peter Plancius. He read everything that other explorers had written about their findings.

Like most seamen at the time, he was quite familiar with Columbus's discovery of America in 1492—more than a hundred years before. That land mass had blocked Columbus's route to China. But Hudson had recently received exciting new information—information that he thought would help him succeed where Columbus had failed.

A letter had come from an old friend, Captain John Smith, in the English settlement at Jamestown, Virginia. Smith's bravery was well-known. He had kept the colony going in the face of hunger, sickness, and death. He had found food for the settlers and made peace with neighboring Indians.

Like Hudson, Captain Smith dreamed of finding a shorter route to the Far East. He had explored Chesapeake Bay and the Susquehanna and Potomac Rivers. None of these routes led to China. So Smith asked the Indians for advice. They told him there was a sea to the north that led to the western ocean. This must be the shortcut!

Captain Smith didn't have the time or money to explore this northwesterly route himself. So he had sent the information to his friend Henry Hudson.

But how could Hudson explore in the New World on this trip? Didn't his contract order him to follow a northern and *eastern* route? He had a plan.

When the *Half Moon* set sail, Captain Hudson took along a secret item, an item he hadn't talked about with his Dutch bosses. It was Captain Smith's letter. This letter, Hudson hoped, would be the answer to all his problems.

The *Half Moon* Sets Sail

W hen the *Half Moon* left Amsterdam on April 4, 1609, it passed by a structure known as the Weeping Tower. Watching from the tower were the wives and friends of the Dutch sailors. They wept as the ship passed by.

In those days, many sailors died at sea. Living in cold, wet clothes, and eating bad food, the crewmen often got sick. Even going to the bathroom was dangerous. A sailor had to squat on two planks that jutted out from the ship's hull. A big wave could knock him into the ocean and drown him.

Sailing was a hard life in other ways, too. Every member of the tiny crew had to "know the ropes." Each line in the ship's rigging had a different name and purpose. In the dark of night, sailors often had to find and adjust these icy ropes, tying special knots to make them tighter. Day and night there was work to be done, from keeping watch to swabbing down the deck. The seaman's life was always full of hardship and danger. But Hudson's trip was bound to be far worse. He was leading his men into the unknown. Perhaps they would never return.

Within a month, the *Half Moon* was sailing north of Norway. It had reached the Arctic Ocean.

If Hudson and the Englishmen were ready for the biting winds, ice, and fog, the Dutch sailors were not. They were used to sailing through hot steamy weather, in the East Indies. The freezing weather must have horrified them. Quarrels and fistfights between the English and Dutch broke out often.

Then the *Half Moon* found its path completely blocked by ice. The crew seemed ready to mutiny. Hudson had to do something, and do it fast.

He called a meeting of everyone onboard. If they returned to Amsterdam now, he said, the trip would be a total failure. Then he took out the letter from Captain John Smith that described a passageway that led all the way through America to China. Hudson told his men that they could find this Northwest Passage. If they did, he promised, the sailors would be richly rewarded—something that didn't happen often.

To Hudson's relief, the seamen agreed. So far, his bold plan had worked. He was breaking his contract with the Dutch East India Company, and he would lose his salary. But he was gaining a chance to fulfill his lifelong dream.

He turned the *Half Moon* around and set his course. They were now headed west toward America.

Getting there at all in one piece was no small feat. Off the coast of Norway, the little ship was caught in an enormous storm. When mighty winds and high waves threatened to sink their ship, Hudson put every man on deck. From the cabin boy to the captain himself, the whole crew struggled to keep the *Half Moon* afloat.

The storm lasted twenty-four hours. But the tiny ship survived.

There would be more storms to come. The next one knocked the foremast right off the ship, and wind ripped the foresail. Still, Hudson bravely sailed on.

As they neared North America, the weather finally turned calm. Now the men could fish. The fish were certainly biting. During one five-hour period, the crew of the *Half Moon* reeled in 118 codfish.

Then, on July 12, the lookout sang out "Land, ho!" In the log, Robert Juet wrote that they saw "a low white sandy ground." Before they could explore, though, the weather turned foggy. They had to wait for the mist to clear.

Several days went by, but the bay was still too misty for the ship to move forward. On the morning of July 17th, the men of the *Half Moon* were still waiting. Then, at 10:00 o'clock, they had visitors.

Two canoes filled with Indians came paddling out of the mist toward the ship. The Indians wore only deerskins. Their dark bodies were smeared with foul-smelling animal grease.

The Indians came on board. They had met white men before. They were used to trading with French fishermen, and even spoke some words of French. They trusted the sailors. But the Dutch and English sailors had never seen Indians before, and they were afraid.

Eager to make friends with the Indians, Hudson gave them food and drink. He also handed out some trinkets that he had brought along to trade for spices in China.

The Indians left happy. But the crew was sure that the Indians meant to kill them.

The next day, the mist finally cleared. The sailors found themselves anchored in a beautiful bay, surrounded by thick forest. They were looking at what we now call Penobscot Bay, Maine. The *Half Moon* had arrived in the New Land.

Hudson immediately sent men ashore in the shallop. They had orders to cut down a tree big enough to replace the *Half Moon*'s missing mast. Over the next few days, the sailors rebuilt their foremast and refilled the ship's water casks. They also caught batches of Maine lobsters—nearly sixty at a time.

While they worked, many more Indians visited the ship. They seemed friendly, but the sailors were still afraid. "The people coming aboard, showed us great friendship," wrote Juet. "But we could not trust them." The sailors kept their weapons handy. Juet believed that was the only reason the Indians didn't attack. "They offered us no wrong seeing we stood upon our guard," he wrote.

As it turned out, the Indians were the ones

who should have been on their guard. Juet and some of the crew were at work on a plan—a plan to attack the Indians.

By the 23rd, the sailors had finished rebuilding their mast. The next night, Juet and his men watched where the Indians put their canoes.

When the sun came up, six sailors rowed to shore.

They stole one of the Indians' boats and brought it back to the ship as a souvenir.

Then twelve sailors crept up on a nearby Indian village, bringing along powerful guns called murderers. These guns fired rocks. They scared the Indians out of their tents. Then the sailors stole whatever they could lay their hands on.

The Indians had done them no harm. But to old Juet, the reason for the raid was simple. The Indians would have done the same thing to them, he said. Juet thought it was smart to attack first. Besides, the sailors believed that the Indians were lowly, unimportant people. What was done to them didn't matter.

But Hudson feared that the angry Indians would seek revenge. He gave orders to raise anchor. The little ship rushed south.

Could This Be It?

The *Half Moon* was sailing down the coast of North America. All seemed well—they had left the Penobscot Indians far behind. Still, the crew was jumpy.

One night the men heard strange and scary noises from shore. It sounded as if Englishmen were crying out for help. Hudson sent some of his crew to explore. But they saw only Indians, and very friendly ones at that.

The men brought one of the Indians back to the boat. Hudson gave him food and three or four glass buttons. Then his men rowed the Indian back.

Hudson had used hand signals to tell the Indian that he wanted to fish. Onshore, the grateful Indian now began waving his arms. He was showing the ship where there was good fishing.

It seemed to the men that there was good fishing everywhere. They soon came to a cape where they caught codfish after codfish. Hudson thought this must be Cape Cod.

Bartholomew Gosnold, another explorer, had named that cape in 1602. But Hudson was a little off in his figuring. The *Half Moon* was now at a different peninsula, Cape Malabar.

It was an easy mistake to make. At that time, nautical instruments were very crude. With only those instruments to use, it's amazing that the seamen found their way around as well as they did!

On the night of August 4, a strange sight startled the sailors on deck. The ship's cat "ran crying from one side of the ship to the other, looking overboard." Alarmed, the sailors stared hard into the night. They couldn't see what had frightened their pet. That didn't calm the sailors, though. The cat's strange behavior seemed like a bad sign. Perhaps their raid on the Penobscot Indians had brought them bad luck.

Hudson headed south again, and the weather soon began to grow warmer. The same crew that had shivered in the Arctic Ocean now sweated in the Atlantic.

By the middle of August, Hudson was off

the coast of Virginia, near the Jamestown Colony. But he didn't stop to visit his friend Captain John Smith. To this day, no one knows why. Fierce storms rocked the *Half Moon* that week, so perhaps the weather kept his ship at sea. Or maybe it was only that Hudson was eager to get on with his search.

He now turned around and began to sail north, hugging the shoreline all the way. He explored every possible water route. The sailor in the crow's nest had orders to sing out at any break in the shoreline. One of these bays or rivers, Hudson believed, would take him to China.

On August 28, the lookout cried out that he had sighted a huge bay. Hudson sailed in, exploring for a day. But the bay soon proved too shallow for the *Half Moon*. The boat sailed on, leaving behind what we now call Chesapeake Bay.

Very early on the morning of September 2, the *Half Moon* anchored offshore in the misty darkness. "We saw a great fire," wrote Juet, "but could not see the land."

When the mist cleared, the crew found themselves anchored off an island that today is called Sandy Hook, New York. Hudson sailed around this island and saw a most exciting sight.

Before him lay a huge bay lined with high cliffs. In the distance a river led inland. Surely this was the Northwest Passage Captain Smith had heard about from the Indians!

It was getting dark. Hudson commanded his men to lower the anchor. He would have to wait till the next morning to explore. But the day dawned cold and misty. It was so misty that Hudson had to wait again. And waiting was hard when he seemed so close.

Finally, at ten o'clock, the mist lifted. Hudson sailed ahead.

He was not the first explorer to come this far. Eighty-five years earlier, Giovanni da Verrazano had sailed into the same bay. But Henry Hudson would be the first to explore the river itself. He would even give it his name. Hudson had begun his most famous journey.

At first the trip was slow going. The *Half Moon* had to wait while the shallop rowed on ahead.

The men in the rowboat had a long line attached to a lead weight. They used this line to measure the depth of the water. As the shallop rowed back and forth in front of the boat, dropping the line again and again, they kept reporting safe depths.

The sailors passed what is now called Staten Island, Coney Island, and Long Island. Each hour, majestic new sights greeted the crew. "Great and tall oaks" lined the shore, Robert Juet wrote. The trees were bigger and taller than any they had ever seen.

The land smelled sweet. The water was full of fish. They caught salmon, mullet, and ray fish so big that it took four of the crew to haul the creatures on board.

Indians paddled out to the *Half Moon*. They had never seen so large a ship, or men with such pale skins. Many of the Indians came aboard. "Some wore mantles of feathers," wrote Juet. Others wore furs and skins. "Women wore copper jewelry around their necks."

They came bearing gifts of tobacco. In return, Hudson gave the natives knives and beads. Some of the sailors went onshore to visit the Indians, who gave them more tobacco and dried currants. The currants were "sweet and good," Juet noted. Still, he insisted, "We dare not trust them." Up ahead the waterway narrowed. Hudson's heart must have sunk at the sight. He had sailed into so many dead ends

already. Once more he sent the shallop up ahead. Four sailors and John Coleman, the first mate, rowed off.

The men in the shallop stopped from time to time to drop the line. On either side of them they saw beautiful grassy shores, colorful flowers, massive trees. And then, they saw the best sight of all.

It looked as if the river led to an open sea. This waterway was looking more and more like the Northwest Passage they were searching for.

Coleman ordered the men to turn around. Excited, they began to row back in a hurry. It was dusk and hard to see. That was when the Indians attacked.

Two huge canoes rushed toward them in the darkness. Fourteen Indians rode in one, twelve in the other. All were armed with bows and arrows. With a whoosh, they let fly. Arrows rained down on the five sailors in the rowboat.

Coleman and his men were rowing as fast as they could, trying to get out of range of the arrows. The men were also trying to load their guns, but it had started to rain. As the men struggled to light their fuses for the gunpowder, the rain put the fuses out.

Meanwhile, the arrows kept falling. One hit

John Coleman in the throat. He died instantly. Two other sailors were badly wounded. Still rowing hard, the two remaining men in the shallop managed to escape into the night.

The darkness protected them. But it also hid the *Half Moon*. The frightened sailors rowed and rowed, searching for their mother ship.

At the same time, Hudson and the crew were looking for the lost shallop. They didn't find it until morning.

The rowboat was a grisly sight. Coleman lay slumped over in the boat, dead. The two wounded men were in very bad shape.

John Coleman was buried ashore. Hudson's crew wanted revenge, but the captain pressed on.

Ambushed!

The *Half Moon* was passing by the mountains now known as the Catskills. Indians came out of the woods to see the strange ship float by. These watchers seemed friendly, but the crew was ready for trouble.

One day some Indians came aboard the ship carrying bows and arrows. Hudson quickly ordered his men to take two of them as prisoners. One escaped by diving off the side of the boat. Before long, the captain saw that the tribe was friendly, and decided to let the other prisoner go as well.

As the trip went on, the crew became a little calmer around the Indians. Hudson and some of his men even went ashore with several of them. According to Hudson, they were treated like kings. "When I came on shore," he wrote, "the swarthy natives all stood around, and sung in their fashion."

The Indians led the explorer and his men back to their campsite. "They had no houses," Hudson wrote, "but slept under the blue heavens, sometimes on mats of bulrushes, and sometimes on the leaves of trees. They always carry with them all their goods, such as their food and green tobacco. . . ."

Another day, a chief of a different tribe took Hudson and some of the sailors to meet his people. The chief led the mariners into a round hut made of oak bark.

"On our coming into the house, two mats were spread out to sit upon. And immediately some food was served in well-made red wooden bowls.

"Two men were also despatched at once with bows and arrows in quest of game, who soon after brought in a pair of pigeons which they had shot. They likewise killed a fat dog, and skinned it in great haste with shells which they had got out of the water.

"They supposed that I would remain with them for the night. But I returned after a short time on board the ship.

"The natives are a very good people," he added. "For when they saw that I would not remain, they supposed that I was afraid of their bows. And taking the arrows, they broke them in pieces, and threw them into the fire."

Hudson was grateful for his meal with the Indians, and he wanted to return the favor. The next time a group of Indians visited, Hudson had his chance.

"He took them down into the cabin," Juet noted in his journal. "And gave them so much wine and Aqua Vitae, that they were all merry. And one of them had his wife with him, which sat so modestly, as any of our country women would do in a strange place."

The Indians had never tasted alcohol before. One older man got so drunk that he fell asleep in the cabin and slept through the night. Alarmed, his fellow Indians returned the next morning to see if he was all right. They were very relieved to see the old man back on his feet again. They then wanted Hudson to come ashore again for dinner. But Hudson had to say no. He didn't want to lose any more time.

The *Half Moon* had sailed far up the river. They had arrived at the site where Albany, New

York, is today. Back then, of course, Hudson saw only forest.

So far the river had been wide and deep. Now the passage narrowed and the water turned shallow. They began sailing up what today is called the Mohawk River. The shallop rowed ahead to check the depth of the water.

The men in the shallop came back looking grim. Up ahead the water was only seven feet deep. The *Half Moon* could go no farther.

Gloom fell over the captain and his crew. Once again they would have to turn back. Once again a route that had seemed so promising proved to be worthless.

The trip up the river had taken most of September. There was little time left for exploring. Hudson had no choice but to turn the *Half Moon* around and head back the way he had come.

Hudson felt that this voyage was another failure. He didn't realize that his trip up the river would make history.

In just a few years, the Dutch East India Company would begin to trade for fur and lumber with the Indians along this river. The Dutch traders would find most of the Indians friendly.

They would set up many trading posts along Hudson's river. In 1626 a Dutchman named Peter Minuit would buy the island of Manhattan from the Indians. He paid them trinkets worth about 60 guilder. For the whole island, he had paid $24.

Minuit made Manhattan the capital of a new Dutch colony. The Dutch called it New Amsterdam. They claimed the land because of Hudson's voyage up the river.

But the English claimed the land too. They pointed out that Hudson was English, even if he had sailed for the Dutch.

In the 1600's, the English and Dutch would fight three wars over the land Hudson had discovered. Finally, in 1664, the English gained control over New Amsterdam and changed its name to New York.

So the discoveries Hudson had made in 1609 led to the founding of one of America's most important colonies. Hudson's "failure" came to be known as his greatest success. Today, Henry Hudson is probably the most famous explorer.

In September of 1609, though, Hudson didn't know about any of this. All he knew was that he had to sail back down the river the way he had come. The trip out would prove to be much bloodier than the trip in.

More Indians came on board the *Half Moon* as they sailed back toward the Atlantic. At first these visits were peaceful. Then, on the first of October, a friendly visit turned violent.

The trouble began when Robert Juet caught an Indian stealing a pillow, two shirts, and some leather ammunition belts from his cabin. He shot and killed the Indian on the spot.

At the sound of gunshots, the rest of the Indians jumped off the ship. Many of the sailors were still furious about the murder of John Coleman. Several of them scrambled into the shallop and rowed after the Indians as they swam away.

When one of the Indians put his hand on the side of the rowboat, a sailor chopped it off with his sword. The Indian disappeared into the depths of the river. But the rest of them got away. The sailors quickly rowed back to the *Half Moon*. Hudson ordered them to raise anchor. The ship sailed as fast as the wind would carry it. They were six miles downriver before darkness fell.

The next day Hudson, afraid that the Indians would strike back, continued to race toward the sea. The mariners put twenty miles more between them and the Indians.

And then it happened. Just around a bend, over a hundred Indians waited on both shores with bows and arrows. As the *Half Moon* sailed by, the Indians jumped out of the woods and began shooting. Others rode out in canoes to get a closer shot.

Hudson's sailors were better armed than the Indians—they shot back with guns. Juet used a small but powerful kind of cannon called a falcon. After he killed several Indians, the rest fled into the woods. Despite the storm of arrows, no sailor had been hurt.

Just when it seemed that the battle was over, the Indians attacked again. Ten more warriors chased the Dutch ship in a canoe. As the Indians shot arrows, sailors fired back with their muskets. Juet blasted the canoe with his falcon. Four more Indians were killed. Soon the larger and faster *Half Moon* had left all the Indians far behind.

They were out of danger. But the crew didn't want to stay and wait for more trouble— they wanted to go home.

Home was the last place Henry Hudson wanted to go. He wanted to keep on exploring until he found the Northwest Passage. But the ship was low on food and other supplies.

The captain may also have felt that he needed a more peaceful crew. This crew would make it hard for him to deal with the Indians. So once again he agreed to head back home.

Hudson could only hope that he would sail again soon. By spring his wish would be granted. In April 1610 the master explorer was back at sea. But this fateful voyage was to be his last.

Bad Omens

On Hudson's way back to Amsterdam, the *Half Moon* stopped in England, docking in Dartmouth on November 7, 1609. When he got to London, Hudson sent a letter to the Dutch East India Company, proposing another trip north. He asked the Dutch to send only 1500 guilders to cover the cost of supplies. He would capture whales to help pay for the rest of the trip. This time, he promised he would sail even farther north. He would find a way past the North Pole at last.

Hudson's letter made the Dutch merchants angry. The *Half Moon* was still docked in England. The merchants wrote back demanding that Hudson return their ship at once. In addition, they hadn't yet received the full report of Hudson's voyage. They wanted to know about his last trip before talking about his next one.

Before Hudson could answer this letter, the English government stepped in. They ordered Hudson to ignore the Dutch company's letter—they would take care of all future business with Holland themselves.

The English knew that Hudson had explored land in the New World. They wanted to keep this land under British control. From now on, they said, Hudson would sail only for his own country.

After the winter, the Dutch sailors from Hudson's voyage sailed back to Amsterdam in the *Half Moon*. The Dutch East India Company finally got its ship back, but they still didn't have the charts and journals of Hudson's voyage. Though they were furious, there was little they could do for the time being.

The Dutch merchants put the *Half Moon* back in their fleet. This sturdy ship would soon start off on new journeys. Over the next few years, it carried sailors on the long trip to the East Indies and back. The *Half Moon* was last reported docked at the Island of Sumatra in 1616. No one knows what happened to the ship after that.

For most mapmakers, Hudson's latest trip had settled an important question. There was no passage existing leading from the Atlantic to the Pacific. But the English still felt that there was one hope left for a shortcut to the East. And it was a dangerous one. This last chance lay beyond the Furious Overfall, a waterway at the entrance to what is now called the Hudson Strait in Northern Canada.

The Overfall had been discovered by the English explorer John Davis in 1585. Exploring far to the north, Davis had found a waterway that looked like a possible shortcut. But here the water swirled, foamed, bubbled, and roared in a terrifying way. Davis had turned back. Some in Britain believed they could find a clear passage to China beyond this whirlpool.

The English merchants had no trouble picking a captain for their exploration. Henry Hudson seemed like the only man for the job. He had tried harder than anyone else to find the Northwest Passage. He knew the waters. Most of all, he seemed to be fearless and tireless in his explorations.

When Captain Hudson agreed to command, the merchants rushed to organize the voyage. They were in a hurry because they feared that the Dutch East India Company might be planning the same trip.

As it turned out, the Dutch weren't planning any such thing—just then they were too disappointed about not receiving Hudson's full report. But the British fear of the Dutch got Hudson back out to sea quickly.

The English merchants had no trouble raising money for the new voyage. Several powerful men were backing them, including the Prince of Wales. And this time Hudson could pick his own crew.

Once again he hired his son John and his loyal carpenter, Philip Staffe. He also hired Robert Juet as first mate. On previous trips Juet had been one of the men who forced Hudson to turn back. But Hudson still trusted the old sailor. He believed that Juet would behave better this time.

Only one member of the crew was not to Hudson's liking. That was his assistant, a man named Coleburne, who had been hired by the merchants. He would not last long.

"The seventeenth of April, 1610," Hudson noted in his journal, "we brake ground." That meant they raised the anchor and were off. Hudson guided his new ship, the *Discovery*, away from St. Katharine's Pool near the Tower of London.

Five days later, Hudson fired Coleburne and sent him home in a small boat. In his journal, Hudson wrote that he also sent a letter to his bosses, explaining why he was sending Coleburne back.

What was Hudson's reason? No one knows for sure, because his letter has never been found. But this much is known—it was a bad mistake. Coleburne's replacement would do a great deal of harm.

In a few days, the *Discovery* docked at Gravesend, England. There Hudson hired a new assistant. The man he brought aboard was Henry Greene, of Kent. Young Greene had been living with the Hudson family for some time, so that the captain knew him and liked him.

But Greene began to cause trouble almost at once. While the ship was docked at Harwich, Greene went ashore. There he got into a fierce argument with a man named Wilkinson. The two men planned to fight a duel. Somehow Hudson was able to get his assistant back on board and sail off before the duel could take place.

The sailors had witnessed Greene's violent temper. They would see more of it before the trip was through.

Hudson and his crew now left England and began the journey north. In eleven days the *Discovery* reached Iceland, and—as usual—fog. Stuck in the cold mist, the sailors had nothing to do but sit and wait. Henry Greene wasn't used to such boredom. To pass the time, he got drunk. Then he got into another argument. This time it was with the ship's doctor, twenty-two-year-old Edward Wilson. The two men soon came to blows.

Sailors who saw the fight thought Greene had started it. But Hudson stood by his assistant. He blamed Wilson. He told the crew that the young doctor had a foul mouth. He said that Wilson would insult anybody, even his best friend. But as far as the men were concerned, Hudson was playing favorites. To them, Greene's fight with Wilkinson had seemed like a bad omen for the voyage. His fight with Wilson was a second dangerous sign. They were about to get a third.

In those days, seamen were very superstitious. The sailors on the *Discovery* believed that evil spirits lived inside the mouths of volcanos. They thought that these spirits spewed out the volcano's fiery, molten rock.

The *Discovery* soon sailed past Iceland's

largest volcano—Mount Hekla. The sailors felt this was the worst omen so far. One of the men, Abacuck Pricket, was keeping a journal. The volcano "cast out much fire," he wrote. He felt this was "a sign of foul weather to come in short time."

Hudson quickly steered the *Discovery* past the volcano. But his men were convinced that bad weather and bad trouble lay ahead. They were right.

"Lousy Bay!"

Bad weather hit almost at once. As the *Discovery* tried to sail away from Iceland, ice blocked them in. Hudson steered back to the safe harbor of a nearby bay.

When he tried to sail out again, the wind began blowing against them. Once more the ship had to fall back into the bay.

Hudson's crew was getting sick of going nowhere in the freezing cold. It was the captain's job to name the new lands they discovered, but the sailors decided to name this bay themselves. They called it Lousy Bay.

But when the sailors went ashore, they found that the bay wasn't so lousy after all. They discovered natural hot tubs—hot pools of water bubbling up from deep underground. "Here all our Englishmen bathed themselves," wrote Pricket. "The water was so hot that it would scald a fowl."

It was June 1 before the *Discovery* could sail out of Lousy Bay. Hudson headed west for Greenland. The men must have been sorry to leave their bubbling hot baths behind.

After a few days at sea, old Robert Juet got drunk. He began calling Henry Greene names. Nobody liked the way Hudson seemed to favor Greene—to them the young man was like a teacher's pet. Now Juet told the men that Greene was the captain's spy. Juet also said that they shouldn't go any farther. He wanted to sail back to Iceland. The drunken first mate threatened to take over the ship.

Some of the crew told Hudson what Juet had said. The captain was so angry he wanted to ship the old sailor back to England. He told the carpenter, Philip Staffe, that he was going to turn the *Discovery* around and sail back to Iceland. There he would place Juet in the boat of some English fishermen who were headed for home. The loyal carpenter calmed Hudson down. Juet had been drunk, after all. Staffe persuaded Hudson to let the first mate stay on board.

On June 4 the *Discovery* arrived at Greenland. They couldn't land, though. The water was too icy. "The land in this part is very mountainous," Pricket wrote. "And full of round hills like to sugar loaves, covered with snow."

Next they passed Desolation Island. At first the place did appear desolate, which means lifeless and lonely. But it didn't stay that way for long. Soon the *Discovery* found itself sailing among a vast pod of whales. Three whales began swimming right at the boat!

Two of these whales swam past the *Discovery*. But the third one decided not to be so helpful—it didn't turn to the side! Just as it got to the ship, it dived down and swam right underneath. The sailors knew that the whale could sink the ship if it wanted to. But "we received no harm," wrote Pricket. "Praised be God."

At last they reached the Furious Overfall. There they were almost trapped in the bubbling current. The whirlpool could have sucked down the entire ship. But Hudson piloted them safely through these dangerous swirling waters.

As a reward, the *Discovery* found itself facing more and more ice. At first only small chunks floated by. Seals sunned and napped on many of these little ice islands. But then the

ship came upon gigantic icebergs. When one of the bergs turned over with a crash, huge waves rose high in the air.

Once again Hudson guided them through the narrow passages between these vast blocks of ice. "Into the ice we put ahead," wrote Pricket, "as between two lands."

Just then a storm struck. The wind was blowing their ship toward still another iceberg. But Hudson was used to ice by now. Thinking fast, he anchored the tiny ship right alongside the biggest berg.

"Some of our men this day fell sick," wrote Pricket. As far as he could tell, they were sick with fear.

The storm passed, but the *Discovery* was in no way out of danger. When Hudson sailed south to try to escape the ice, the ice only got thicker. "The more he strove, the worse he was, and the more enclosed," wrote Pricket. "Till we could go no further.

"Here our master was in despair. And, as he told me after, he thought he should never have got out of this ice, but there have perished."

Henry Hudson didn't tell his men that he was worried because he didn't want to scare them. They were terrified enough as it was. Everyone remembered how Captain Hugh Willoughby's ship had been frozen in the ice. The sailors wanted to turn back and head home at once.

Hudson called a hurried meeting of the entire crew. He showed them where they were on his charts. He believed they had gone a hundred leagues farther north than any other English explorer. If only they could go just a little farther, Hudson said, the weather would begin to turn warm again.

Hudson put the decision to a vote. Who wanted to sail on, and who wanted to go back?

"Whereupon," Pricket wrote, "some of the sailors were of one mind and some of another. Some wishing themselves at home, and some not caring where they were. So long as they were out of the ice."

"If I had a hundred pounds, I'd give fourscore and ten to be at home," said one seaman. He felt it would be worth ninety of his hundred pounds to be safely back in England.

Henry's loyal carpenter, Philip Staffe, was quick to answer him. "If I had a hundred pounds, I would not give the money upon any such condition. Because I have confidence that we'll get home."

Old Robert Juet doubted that they could even make it out of the ice, which was thickening all around them. There was little time left for talk.

Still Hudson wasn't giving up. He didn't want to turn back until he found a route to the Far East. But he needed the sailors' support. Finally, with Philip Staffe's help, the captain persuaded his crew to sail on.

Before they could go anywhere, they had to get out of the ice. Hudson and his men worked hard to free the ship. After many hours they cleared enough room for the ship to turn slightly.

"And so by little and little," wrote Pricket, the sailors were able to get clear and sail away.

The voyage went on. But the sailors had had a terrible scare. They didn't forget it.

Juet's Trial

The ship was near Akpatok Island, north of present-day Labrador and just at the entrance to what is now known as Hudson Bay. Some of the crew spotted a bear napping on a floating block of ice. The ship chased after it, but the swift current carried the sleeping bear safely away.

Then another bear began to make its way toward the *Discovery*. The huge animal lumbered from ice block to ice block. It used the ice as stepping stones to help it cross the water. "But when she saw us look at her," wrote Pricket, "she cast her head between her hinder legs and then dived under the ice."

The men were disappointed. Two good chances for food had been lost.

Hudson tried to bring the ship to shore. It wasn't easy. The water was shallow, and jagged rocks lurked under the surface. These rocks could gouge a hole in the ship's bottom and sink it.

Hudson finally found a safe harbor. He named it the Isles of God's Mercy. He sent Abacuck Pricket and another sailor named Thomas Woodhouse ashore to look for game. But they found the land barren, the ground covered with split rock and puddles. Pricket thought earthquakes had occurred there.

Then the two mariners spotted a flock of partridges. They aimed and shot, but hit only one old bird. After a long day of hunting, the two men returned to the ship with only their one puny catch.

The crew was growing more frightened. They needed supplies. What if they got stuck in the frozen north all winter? There wouldn't be enough food to last.

For the next few weeks, the *Discovery* sailed blindly through fields of ice. As soon as he could, Hudson sent another group of men ashore. He put Abacuck Pricket and Philip Staffe in charge of the hunt.

As the men set off, their spirits began to rise. Grass covered this land, not rock. It was the best grass Pricket had seen since

England. This was a hopeful sign. With all this grass to eat, there might well be animals nearby.

Sure enough, a herd of sixteen deer galloped past the sailors. They all fired their muskets, but every deer got away.

After that, the men wandered aimlessly. They didn't see another living creature. However, they did come upon a very strange sight. Before them stood stone mounds, shaped like little huts. The sailors hadn't seen any people, but these stone piles certainly looked man-made.

Pricket lifted the top stone off one of the mounds and looked inside. The mound was hollow. Inside, a long row of fowls had been hung on a stick. The men had struck gold. Eskimos had built these mounds to store their game for the winter. There was more than enough food to refill the ship's larders. They were saved!

Pricket and the other sailors began loading fowl into the shallop. Offshore, they could see the *Discovery*. The boat was sailing closer.

Someone on board fired a shot—a signal from Captain Hudson. A fog was coming in, and he wanted his men back on board.

The sailors rowed back to the ship and showed Hudson the fowl. They asked if they could stay a few days longer so they could load up the whole ship with food.

Hudson refused. He was in too much of a hurry. The days were growing shorter, and he wanted to get through the Northwest Passage before winter. After that, he hoped, the ship would be well on its way to the Orient. There wasn't a moment to lose.

The sailors begged Hudson to wait. They didn't share his confidence that they would soon be in China. The ship's larders were already beginning to run low. What could be more important than food? But the captain gave orders to sail on.

For the next few weeks, the crew saw nothing but ice. Then, on September 10, old Robert Juet called a meeting. It was up to Hudson to call such meetings—the first mate didn't have the right to do it. But Juet insisted, and the men gathered around.

Juet began by saying why he had assembled the crew. He said he wanted to address "some abuses and slanders against himself." He had heard that the captain was calling him a grumbler, and saying he was disloyal. Also that Hudson claimed if the first mate mutinied, it would ruin them all. Juet wanted to set the record straight.

Hudson turned the tables on him. Though Juet had called the meeting, Hudson now took charge. He turned the meeting into Juet's trial. He called witness after witness. He made each witness swear on the Bible that he was telling the truth.

Many sailors stated that it was Juet who had been saying nasty things about Hudson. The captain had promised the men that they would reach the East Indies by February. Juet had been telling everyone that Hudson's promise was a joke.

The carpenter, Philip Staffe, and a sailor named Lodlo Arnold gave harsher evidence. Juet had urged them to keep their muskets loaded and swords ready in their cabins. He wanted them to be ready for a mutiny.

The captain had heard enough. Talking about mutiny was a very serious crime. He fired Juet as first mate. A sailor named Robert Billet would take his place. But Hudson didn't punish Juet any further. He just warned the old sailor to behave himself from now on. If Juet would stay loyal, Hudson promised to forgive him for everything.

But as the awful weather continued, it was old Juet who couldn't forgive the captain. Juet felt that by refusing to turn back, Hudson was risking the lives of everyone on the ship.

A Miserable Winter

Hudson and his crew were used to hardships at sea. On this trip, though, it seemed as if there were nothing but hardships. Everything kept going wrong. Those bad omens from early in the voyage seemed to be coming true.

For eight straight days there had been dreadful storms "thick and foul." The dreadful weather kept the *Discovery* from moving forward.

The crew didn't want to move forward—they wanted to go home. Winter was coming, and winter could mean death for all. But the captain was set on not turning back, no matter what. He had already been forced to turn around without reaching his goal too many times!

As the boat shuddered through day after day of storm, the mood onboard worsened. After eight days, Hudson could stand the wait no longer. Though the storm had not yet stopped, Hudson ordered his men to raise the anchor. Storm or no storm, he would sail ahead.

The sailors objected. They said it was too dangerous. Huge waves were crashing against the sides of the *Discovery*, and freezing rain was pelting down. It wasn't safe to be on deck. But Hudson insisted.

So the men began the job of reeling in the ship's heavy anchor. It was on the end of a thick cable attached to a sort of spool called a capstan. To lift the anchor, the men turned a crank that wound the cable around the capstan.

As they started to work, a giant wave hit the deck and knocked them all down. Now no one was holding the crank. The anchor dropped back into the sea, and the cable wound off the capstan in a fury.

Thinking quickly, Philip Staffe chopped the cable with his ax. The anchor would have been lost anyway. But now there would be enough cable left for the ship's other anchor.

That saved the cable. But it didn't help the sailors who had been knocked to the deck. One of them, Adam Moore, was hurt badly. He soon died. In his obsession with reaching China,

Hudson had made a very bad decision. Trying to sail in the storm had cost the life of one of his crew.

After the storm, the *Discovery* landed. Hudson sent men ashore, where they saw human footprints. That was a good sign. Eskimos must be nearby. If the sailors knew where, they could trade with them for food.

But the men couldn't find them. They didn't find any live game, either. They remembered the fowl in those stone mounds. Hudson had refused to let them stay and restock their larders. If it hadn't been for him, the crew would now have plenty of food.

But Hudson continued to sail ahead. He kept up a furious pace. One night he even set sail at midnight, in the pitch darkness.

Philip Staffe was studying the ship's route. He told Hudson that "if he kept that course he would be upon the rocks."

Hudson refused to listen. To find out if his carpenter was right, he would have had to wait until daylight. And Hudson was no longer willing to wait.

Suddenly there was an ugly scraping sound below. They had hit rocks, just as Staffe had warned. Luckily, they didn't spring a leak. But the ship's bottom had been scarred. It took the sailors twelve hours to move their ship off those rocks and back to sea. As they worked, the crew had yet another reason to be angry at their captain.

The sailors could see that by now Hudson wanted to find the Northwest Passage no matter what. He seemed to care not at all about the crew's safety. Hudson was no longer interested in calming the crew—he just didn't want them to get in his way. So he rounded up all the men's journals. Without them, the sailors could not keep track of the ship's location. If Hudson said they were almost through the ice, no one could say it wasn't so.

Then the captain fired Robert Billet. As first mate he chose his loyal carpenter, Philip Staffe. The crew liked Staffe, but they knew that he had had no formal education. He couldn't read or write, so he would be unable to read Hudson's charts or keep a log. With Staffe as first mate, only Hudson would know where they were headed. The crew didn't like that at all.

It was now the end of October. Winter had set in. For three months now, the ship had been wandering blindly through the icy fog. Pricket wrote that it was like spending "three months in a labyrinth without end." The crew kept saying that they would be stuck here all winter. Now Hudson finally admitted it was true. They were running out of time to look for a safe spot to spend the winter.

On the first of November, the *Discovery* made it to what seemed a safe harbor. They got there just in time. Nine days later, the crew's worst fears came true—they were now in the same position as Captain Willoughby and his men. The ship was frozen in the ice.

The sailors took stock of what was in the ship's store. There was only enough food to last them six months at the most. Hudson offered a reward to anyone killing beast, fish, or fowl. He hoped they could shoot down some of the birds flying overhead.

The cold got worse. The men fell ill easily. Years later Pricket remembered that the cold "lamed most of our company, and myself do yet feel it."

No one was sicker than a sailor named John Williams. Doctors in those days knew few remedies, and Edward Wilson, the ship's surgeon, could not help him. In the middle of November, Williams died.

When a sailor died at sea, it was the custom to sell off his belongings in an auction. All the money raised was saved for the sailor's family back home. Before Williams's auction, Henry Greene went to the captain with a special request—he wanted Williams's gray coat.

Hudson agreed to sell it to Greene. And when other sailors asked about the coat, Hudson told them that Greene would get it and nobody else. Hudson was still playing favorites, which made the crew even angrier at Hudson than they already were.

Philip Staffe, meanwhile, was having his own troubles with Hudson. For days the carpenter had been saying that it was time to build a winter shelter onshore. When Hudson finally agreed, Staffe said it was too late—the wind and cold were too strong. A shelter would be impossible to build.

Like the rest of the icebound crew, Hudson's nerves were on edge. When he heard that Staffe had said no, he was livid. He got the carpenter out of his cabin and called him every foul name he could think of. He even threatened to hang him. Staffe took the abuse without a word.

The next day Staffe went hunting onshore. Hudson had given orders that no man was to risk going ashore alone. For safety reasons, they had to travel in pairs. So young Greene offered to hunt with Staffe.

When Hudson heard that Greene had gone ashore with Staffe, he was furious. Greene knew that Hudson had yelled at the carpenter only the day before. To Hudson, it seemed disloyal for his favorite sailor to act so friendly to Staffe the very next day.

Hudson picked up the gray coat he had promised to Greene and gave it instead to Robert Billet, one of the other sailors who had wanted it. When Greene came back on board, he heard what had happened. He went straight to the captain. You broke your promise, he said.

The crew stood watching. Would Hudson allow his own assistant to talk to him this way? Hudson did not. For the first time in the voyage he yelled at Greene. He shouted that Greene would get no wages. If Greene's friends wouldn't trust him with twenty shillings, cried Hudson, why should he?

Greene was a haughty young man. He couldn't stand being embarrassed in front of the crew. At the time, he made no answer to Hudson's insults. But he had an answer for him later. It was young Greene who would lead a mutiny.

Mutiny!

At last the *Discovery* had some good fortune—large flocks of white birds began flying over the icebound ship. The men were able to shoot enough of them to keep their stomachs full.

But then the birds disappeared.

"We went into the woods, hills, and valleys," Abacuck Pricket wrote, "for all things that had any show of substance in them, howsoever vile." The starving sailors ate moss, which Pricket said tasted worse than sawdust. They ate frogs, which Pricket found "loathsome."

Thomas Woodhouse came upon a tree with buds one could eat. Inside each bud was a gooey substance. Wilson, the boat's surgeon, cooked the goo into a hot drink. He also used the hot buds to treat the sailors' bruises, aches, and pains. Thanks to the buds, wrote Pricket, "I received great and present ease of my pain."

But the men couldn't live on tree buds. As the winter months passed into spring, the fear and anger on board the ship continued to build.

By June the ice had finally begun to break up. But the ship still couldn't sail, and the food supply was running lower and lower.

Then one day an Eskimo visited the ship. Hudson was excited to see him. He hoped to trade trinkets for some food. He gave the Eskimo a knife, a looking glass, and some buttons. The man couldn't speak any English, but he made signs to show that he would come back after one night's sleep.

Sure enough, the man returned the next day, pulling a sled behind him. He had brought deer skins, but still no food. When Hudson gave him more trinkets, the Eskimo made the same signs as before. The sailors watched and waited for his return. But he never came back.

Once the crew spotted a fire onshore. Hudson sent men to search for Eskimos. By now the ice had broken up enough for the men to row off in the shallop. But they searched without success—no Eskimos and no food.

For the starving crew of the *Discovery*, this was just about the last straw. It was time to turn back, they told Hudson. It was spring, and the water was free enough of ice to sail.

Once again Hudson's men hinted at mutiny if the captain didn't listen. When Hudson finally announced that he would turn back, the sailors made him sign a statement. Like the one before, it said that Hudson was returning of his own free will. The crew didn't want to be accused of mutiny when they got home.

As Hudson signed the document, he began to weep. Once again he would have to return home without having found his passage. It was the last thing in the world he wanted to do.

Though Hudson had agreed to head for home right away, for the next few days the *Discovery* stayed right where it was. It seemed as if the captain just couldn't bring himself to turn back.

The food supplies had just about run out, and the crew was furious with Hudson. Many believed that he was hoarding some of the food—that he was keeping more for himself.

He wasn't. He was just trying to help his crew make the small amounts of food last longer. But since the sailors were so upset, Hudson now gave out all the remaining bread.

Many ate it too quickly. One sailor who ate his whole supply of bread at once was sick for three days.

Next Hudson gave out all the cheeses. Still, some of the men kept saying that the captain was hoarding food. Hudson knew he wasn't, but he had an idea who might be. He called for Nicholas Sims, his young cabin boy.

Hudson warned Sims that he would punish anyone who hoarded bread. He also said he was about to break open everyone's locker. The cabin boy asked him to wait. Soon he was back with a bag of thirty loaves.

But even with this bread, there was only enough food left for fourteen days. The sailors were sick, hungry, frozen with cold and fear.

On the night of June 21, some of the seamen decided they could wait no longer. They felt that Hudson wouldn't save them, and they set out to save themselves.

That night Abacuck Pricket was too sick to leave his cabin, so the mutineers came to him. Pricket's first visitors were Henry Greene and a William Wilson. They hadn't eaten anything in three days, they said. They were going to lead a mutiny.

According to Pricket, the two men promised that "What they had begun, they would go through with . . . or die."

The two men especially wanted Pricket to join them. Back in London, he had worked as a servant for the merchants who were paying for the trip. If Pricket joined the mutiny, perhaps the merchants wouldn't punish them so harshly.

Pricket later claimed that he had tried to talk Greene and Wilson out of it. There is no way to know if this was true. Pricket's record of the mutiny is the only one that has ever been found. If he was lying, no one will ever know.

Pricket said that he reminded the two men of the usual penalty for mutiny—hanging. The mutineers could never go back to England. For William Wilson, that would mean never again seeing his wife and children.

"Hold your peace," Greene told Pricket. The worst punishment, he said, was to be hanged. Since he was already starving to death, he "would rather be hanged at home than starved abroad."

Pricket refused to take part in the mutiny. Greene left in a rage, promising to cut the throat of any man who got in his way.

Pricket tried to talk William Wilson into

stopping the plan. It was too late, Wilson told him—there was no turning back now. Greene soon returned, demanding to know if Pricket had changed his mind. "He is in his old song, still patient," answered Wilson.

Pricket then begged young Greene to wait just three more days. He promised that in that time he would convince Henry Hudson to turn the ship around, that there was no need to mutiny. But Greene refused.

Pricket asked for two days. Greene still refused. Pricket then asked for just twelve hours.

"There is no way," answered Greene and Wilson together. Their only question was this: would Pricket join them?

At last, Pricket agreed. He took out a Bible. He made the two men swear an oath that they would not hurt anyone. They both swore.

Soon Pricket's cabin grew crowded with mutineers. First came old Robert Juet, who was still angry at Hudson for firing him as first mate. Then came John Thomas, Michael Perce, Adrian Moter, and Bennet Mathews, the cook. As each mutineer arrived, Pricket had him place a hand on the Bible and declare, "I swear truth to God, my prince and country. I shall do nothing but to the glory of God and the good of the action in hand, and harm to no man."

Then the men ate some bread that they had hoarded. They would need their strength. Next they took their places. The mutiny was about to begin.

On the morning of June 23, the cook, Bennet Mathews, went to the quartermaster, John King, to ask for water.

The ship's supply of fresh water had run very low. It was the quartermaster's job to guard the precious water and make sure no one took too much. King now went down into the ship's hold to get water for the cook.

As soon as he disappeared below, Mathews shut the hatch on him, locking him in. Then he joined Henry Greene, William Wilson, and John Thomas.

The four mutineers waited outside the captain's cabin. When Hudson came out, they all jumped him at once. Mathews and Thomas pinned the captain's arms behind his back, while Wilson tied him up.

"What do you mean to do?" Hudson demanded.

"You'll find out when you're in the shallop," Greene replied.

Now old Juet went down into the hold to fetch John King. But the quartermaster had found a sword, and tried to defend himself.

Juet called to his fellow mutineers, who came down to help. Soon they were able to drag King up on deck, where they tied him up beside his captain.

Bound, Henry Hudson called out for his loyal carpenter, Philip Staffe, but received no answer. Next he called for Abacuck Pricket. Sick and lame with frostbite, Pricket hobbled out of his cabin and called back a reply from the hatchway.

"Robert Juet will overthrow us all," Hudson yelled.

"Nay," Pricket shouted back. "It is that villain Henry Greene!"

Now Greene himself came up on deck. He ordered the shallop put in the water. Then he decreed that all the sick sailors except Pricket be forced out of their cabins. Five of them were loaded into the tiny rowboat.

Philip Staffe finally appeared on deck. If you go through with this, he warned Greene, you'll be hanged.

But Greene surprised him. Although the carpenter was one of Hudson's closest allies, Greene offered to keep him onboard. He may have figured that Staffe could help them steer home. Greene was offering to spare Staffe's life. But standing beside Staffe was Henry Hudson, his arms bound with rope—the man whom he had served on four long voyages. The brave carpenter answered Greene that he would not leave his captain—he would go in the rowboat. Then he went down to say good-bye to Pricket.

Pricket tried to convince the carpenter to stay on board. He said that Staffe could help him convince the mutineers to take Hudson back. Pricket reasoned that they would soon need Hudson—that they would find it too hard to steer the ship home without him.

Again Philip Staffe refused. He had made up his mind. He would not leave Hudson.

He told Pricket that they would try to keep the shallop close to the mother ship. Then he said farewell, and both men wept.

Now Staffe took his place in the shallop with Henry Hudson, John King, the five sick sailors, and the captain's son John. Henry Greene cut the shallop's rope and pushed the boat away.

Greene set sail as fast as he could. The nine men in the small boat tried to row after the *Discovery*, but there was no way they could keep up. Soon the rowboat became a tiny speck on the waves. And then it was gone from sight.

No one in the rowboat was ever seen again—not the sailors or their captain Henry Hudson.

"The Tragical End"

Calling himself the Captain now, Henry Greene ordered his men to ransack the *Discovery*. The sailors had always believed that Henry Hudson was hoarding food. Now they rampaged through the ship, prying open locked chests, breaking into storage rooms.

They found no food. Just as Hudson had said, there was almost nothing left. Only twenty-seven pieces of pork were left in the larder, only half a bushel of peas.

Greene and Juet had no idea how to read Hudson's charts, so they couldn't decide which direction they should sail. Though he had made himself Captain, Greene asked Pricket to move into Hudson's old quarters. The mutineers needed Pricket's help in reading the maps and steering the ship.

The mutiny was off to a bad start. They were still starving, and now they were lost.

When seven boatloads of Eskimos paddled toward the *Discovery*, the men felt saved. The Eskimos were the mutineers' last hope for food.

To be safe, Greene traded a man with the Eskimos. The sailors kept one native on board, while the Eskimos took an English sailor back to their tents. Only then did Greene begin to trade.

As before, the Eskimos had no food with them. But they promised with hand signals that they would bring the sailors deer.

Soon both the sailor and the Eskimo were returned to their groups. When the Eskimos saw their man coming back unharmed, "they made great joy," wrote Pricket, "dancing and leaping and stroking their breasts."

Greene then decided that the Eskimos meant them no harm. He even told his men that they could stop standing guard. He and a small group headed ashore in the ship's second rowboat to trade for deer.

As they rowed toward the shore, they could see the Eskimos standing on the snowy hills. When the rowboat landed, Greene and Michael

Perce stepped out. Then the Eskimos attacked.

They came at the two sailors from all sides, bearing broad knives with handles made of walrus tusks. Greene had a club and Perce had a hatchet, but they were badly outnumbered.

The Eskimos also attacked the men in the rowboat. One Eskimo stabbed Abacuck Pricket several times before Pricket could grab his hand. They wrestled in the boat. During the struggle, Pricket managed to take out his own knife and kill his attacker. Then Greene and Perce "came tumbling into the boat together."

"Coraggio!" cried Henry Greene as he swung his club. This is an Italian word meaning courage.

The sailors struggled to pull their boat back into the water. As they began to row back to the *Discovery*, the Eskimos were shooting arrows from shore.

One arrow struck Pricket in the back. Another hit Henry Greene. Wounded, Michael Perce fainted, slumping over the oars.

Adrian Moter stood up in the rowboat as the arrows whistled around him. He waved wildly at the *Discovery*. But Greene had told the crew to leave their watch.

Finally, the sailors saw Moter and sailed in

to save the shallop. By then, the men in the boat had rowed out of arrow range, but it was too late. Henry Greene was dead. Except for Pricket, all the others died soon after.

And this, wrote Pricket, was "the tragical end of Henry Greene and his mates, whom they called captain."

The bloody battle with the Eskimos left only nine men on board the *Discovery*. All were sick and hungry, so hungry that they ate almost anything.

The sailors tried to make it to Ireland. They thought that was the closest place they could find food. They were so weak with hunger "that they could not stand at the helm"—they had to sit as they steered the ship.

They were in despair. They had no food left, and very litle hope. Then the nine men became eight. Old Juet had died of hunger.

"A sail! A sail!"

The joyous cry came from one of the sailors on deck. He had spotted some Irish fishermen. The *Discovery* had made it to Ireland's Bay of Galway. The last eight mutineers were saved.

The sailors filled their stomachs and restocked the ship's larder. Then they sailed on to London. When they arrived, they told the merchants what had happened to Hudson. The Prince of Wales sent boats out to hunt for the great explorer. But they searched without success.

The surviving men had committed the worst of crimes—mutiny and murder. But they weren't put on trial for five years. Why did it take so long?

These eight sailors were the only men alive who knew what Hudson had discovered on his trip. The English merchants who paid for the voyage wanted their help in guiding other explorers. Before they were put on trial, some of the men actually sailed again.

Finally, though, all eight mutineers stood trial back in London. The High Court of Admiralty found all of them guilty, even the cabin boy, Nicholas Sims. What punishment they were given is not known.

Henry Hudson was never seen or heard from again. But he was far from forgotten. His daring showed future explorers the way to the North Pole. The bay where he spent his last winter is now known as Hudson Bay. Hudson's travels had led to the settling of New York, and the river he explored is named for him.

In fact, Hudson's name appears all over New York State. In Manhattan today, the highway that runs along the Hudson River is called the Henry Hudson Parkway. Manhattan is also home to a Hudson Street and a Hudson Park branch of the public library. In upstate New York there's a Hudson city and in New Jersey a Hudson county.

But his fame is not limited to North America. Almost four hundred years after his death, people throughout the world know the name Henry Hudson. That name stands for daring and for bravery. It stands for a master explorer.

Highlights in the Life of
Henry Hudson

April 19, 1607

Captain Henry Hudson leaves London in the *Hopewell* with a daring plan—to sail through the North Pole to China.

June 27, 1607

Hudson discovers vast numbers of whales off the Islands of Spitsbergen, a finding that later gives birth to the huge British whaling industry.

April 22, 1608

Hudson again sets sail in the *Hopewell*, this time searching for a sea route even farther east of the North Pole.

July, 1608

Hudson finds his route blocked with ice, and a near mutiny by the crew forces him to turn back.

September, 1608

British merchants refuse to back Hudson on a new trip, so he travels to Amsterdam to meet with the Dutch East India Company. He hopes to convince them to send him to the North Pole once more.

January 8, 1608

Hudson signs a contract with the Dutch to search for a shortcut to China.

April 4, 1609

Hudson sets sail from Amsterdam in a tiny ship, the *Half Moon*.

May, 1609

Sailing toward the Pole, Hudson again finds his way blocked by ice. Although the crew wants to return home, Hudson convinces them to sail on with him to North America. There he hopes to find the Northwest Passage, a river leading from the Atlantic to the Pacific—and straight to China.

July 12, 1609

The *Half Moon* lands in Penobscot Bay, Maine. The sailors meet their first Indians, who are friendly and want to trade.

September 3, 1609

Hudson comes upon a great expanse of water—Lower New York Bay—that seems to lead into the land for miles. He begins his most famous trip, sailing up the river that today bears his name. To his great disappointment, he finds the river does not lead to the Pacific.

April 17, 1610

Hudson sails from England aboard the *Discovery*, once more searching for a route past the North Pole.

November 10, 1610

The *Discovery* finds itself in Hudson Bay, frozen in the ice for the winter, and dangerously low on food.

June 23, 1610

Hudson's assistant, Henry Greene, turns traitor and leads a mutiny. Hudson and eight others loyal to him are left in a tiny rowboat, never to be seen or heard from again.

CELEBRATING
YEARLING
25 YEARS